DATE DUE

DEMCO 128-8155

**Everything
You Need to
Know About**

Bipolar Disorder and Manic-Depressive Illness

Greek physician Hippocrates (460 BC–377 BC) is known
as the founder of medicine. He thought the body must
be treated as a whole and not just as a series of parts.

Everything You Need to Know About

Bipolar Disorder and Manic-Depressive Illness.

Michael A. Sommers

The Rosen Publishing Group, Inc.
New York

To Jesse, who had to deal with a lot of depressed people

Published in 2000, 2003 by The Rosen Publishing Group, Inc.
29 East 21st Street, New York, NY 10010

Revised Edition 2003

Library of Congress Cataloging-in-Publication Data

Sommers, Michael.
Everything you need to know about bipolar disorder and manic-depressive illness / by Michael Sommers.
p. cm. — (The need to know library)
Includes bibliographical references and index.
ISBN 0-8239-3768-2
1. Manic-depressive illness—Juvenile literature. 2. Manic-depressive illness in adolescence—Juvenile literature. [1. Manic-depressive illness. 2. Mental illness.] I. Title. II. Series.
RC516 .J684 2001
616.89'5—dc21
2001001311

Manufactured in the United States of America

Contents

*I*ntroduction

Depression has been around since the beginning of human history. In biblical times, Saul, who became the first king of Israel, suffered from severe mood swings. His servants hired a harpist, hoping the sweet music would soothe him. The harpist was a young shepherd named David, who became a favorite at the king's house. Later, David became a big hero for killing the giant Goliath. Saul was so jealous of David's popularity that his depression returned. Saul plotted to kill David. His hostility led to a war in which he and his sons were killed, leaving David as the king of Israel.

In the fifth century BC, a Greek doctor named Hippocrates treated patients who had melancholia, a "humor," or mood disorder, that left people feeling "sleepless, irritable and restless." Centuries later, in the 1600s, Prince Hamlet, the moody title character in William Shakespeare's play *Hamlet*, spoke these bleak words:

How weary, stale, flat and unprofitable
Seem to me all the uses of this world.

Although few people are aware of this, U.S. president Abraham Lincoln was so troubled by depression in the mid-nineteenth century that he described himself as "the most miserable man living."

Today, depression is just as painful and destructive. It affects people of all ages, nationalities, religions, and races. There are various types of depression. One of the most frequent and complex is manic depression, known to professionals as bipolar disorder. The prefix "bi," which means two, refers to the two moods of bipolar disorder, and the ending "polar" refers to the opposite states or poles that characterize the illness. So bipolar disorder is a condition that causes your mood to swing back and forth between two opposite emotional states.

This means that you experience periods of major depression in which you feel sad, lonely, weak, and helpless. Other times you have manic periods in which you feel energetic and confident. You can experience extreme sensations of anger, irritation, or happiness. Your mood might go from low and despairing (during the depressed phase) to elated—extremely happy—and hypersensitive (during the manic phase), and then back to low and despairing again. Because these phases are so radically different and are often interspersed with seemingly "normal" periods, bipolar disorder can be difficult to diagnose. Take, for example, the case of Lucy.

Lucy first began feeling strange after her thirteenth birthday. At times she heard a buzzing in her head that made her irritable. At home she snapped at her parents, whose comments she thought were stupid and boring. Meanwhile, school was slowly becoming intolerable. Teachers droned on and on and classes seemed neverending. They were so tiresome that she wanted to scream. Sometimes, Lucy felt as if she were screaming in her head.

By the time she entered high school, Lucy had stopped doing her homework and had begun cutting classes. For nights at a time, she could not sleep. Her behavior was very irregular.

Once, during a sleepless night, she decided that she did not have any interesting clothes. She pulled all of her clothes out of her closet and threw them on the floor. The next day, she stole her mother's credit card and went on a crazy buying spree.

After the second time Lucy stole her mother's credit card, her mother threatened to kick her out of the house. By then, Lucy wasn't getting along with her parents at all. Any discussion led to a massive fight, with Lucy screaming hysterically.

Even Lucy's friends thought she was acting weird. They stopped inviting her out with them. "What's with you?" they asked her. "How come you're acting so strange? You've been really irritable lately."

Lucy had been feeling increasingly annoyed with everybody. She didn't know what was wrong with her. She felt alone and did not know where to turn. Everybody seemed to be against her.

Lucy thought that she heard whispering behind her back. The whispers joined the buzzing in her head, and at times she felt as if she were going crazy. Nights were the worst. She was so nervous that she sneaked out of the house and went for long walks. If she stayed at home, she would jump out of her skin. On her walks, Lucy discovered some after-hours bars that would serve minors. She would drink a few beers, hoping that this would help to relax her, but it didn't seem to work. She started drinking harder stuff, such as tequila and gin.

Lucy was barely showing up at school. The school principal finally had a talk with her parents about how difficult she had become. The principal wondered if there was something wrong at home. Afterward, Lucy's parents were furious. "Why are you acting like this?" her mother demanded. Her dad yelled at her, "You're ruining your life!"

Lucy tried to turn over a new leaf. For a while, things seemed OK. She went back to school and tried to pay attention. At night, with her parents watching over her, she tried to do homework. Her friends still ignored her. Nobody understood. Everything was becoming too much of an effort. She was still drinking, only now it was not to relax but because she needed a pick-me-up.

Then Lucy crashed. One day, shortly after she started walking to school, Lucy turned around and went home. All she wanted to do was to stay in bed and cry. She had never felt so useless and miserable in all her life. When her parents saw her in this state, they realized that Lucy was not just a rebellious teenager acting up. They realized that she had a problem and that she needed help.

Lucy's mother talked with the counselor at Lucy's school and with the family doctor. Both said it sounded as if Lucy was suffering from some kind of depression. They recommended that Lucy and her parents see a psychiatrist. Lucy did not want to see anybody. She had never felt so low. It seemed impossible that anyone would be able to help her or that she would ever feel better. Her parents pleaded with her. They finally got angry and yelled at her. Lucy didn't care. She felt as if she had plunged into the bottom of a well and couldn't climb out.

Chapter 1

What Is Bipolar Disorder?

As do adults, most teens go through periods when they feel sad or blue. At these times, you may slam the door to your room and feel like hiding your head under the pillows. Maybe you do not feel like talking to your parents or hanging out with your friends. You might be feeling angry or irritated. Maybe you think of yourself as a loser. Sometimes these feelings are reactions to a problem. Perhaps you are sick with a bad case of the flu, you're having some trouble at school, or your best friend is mad at you. Within a week or two, you will probably start to feel a little better.

However, depression is a disease. Although feelings of depression come and go, the disease of depression can stay around and get worse. Just as with diabetes or bronchitis, depression can get worse if left untreated by a professional. Depression affects your emotional state, leaving you exhausted or panicky, teary or desperate. It also affects your physical well-being.

11

Depressed people often feel constantly tired. They may experience headaches and stomachaches or uncontrollable shaking and fidgeting.

According to the American Psychiatric Association (APA), one out of every five Americans will experience serious depression during his or her lifetime. Sadly, the APA estimates that the majority of depressed people fail to recognize the illness and get help. If they stop eating regularly and feel constantly worried, these people blame it on stress. If they can't think straight, they believe it's because they don't get enough sleep. If they feel tired and achy, they think that they must have some kind of bug. In the meantime, the real problem—depression—stays unresolved and often gets worse.

Teens and Depression

For a long time, it was thought that only adults could be victims of major depression. In fact, there are increasing numbers of teens who are affected by depression. According to the National Institute of Mental Health (NIMH), of the 18 million Americans who are depressed, up to an estimated 2 million are teenagers. Some mental health experts think that as many as 20 percent of high school students are very unhappy or suffer from a mood disorder.

Teenage years are filled with change, so it is natural to experience a lot of ups and downs. You suddenly

Depression not only affects you emotionally, but also physically with symptoms such as nausea, stomach pain, and fatigue.

have new pressures to cope with as you try to come to terms with your changing attitudes toward your parents, friends, and teachers. Some of the new things you are dealing with will be confusing. Why do you feel furious when your best buddy starts to spend a lot of time with his new girlfriend? Why does the size of your growing breasts make you so embarrassed that you start cutting school to get out of gym class?

It is important to let people you trust know how you are feeling and what you are going through. Adults sometimes make the mistake of seeing teens as naturally moody. They will say things such as "You are in your terrible teens," or "You're just going through a difficult phase." This is why it is often hard to detect depression in teens and why real problems are easily ignored.

Manic Depression

Generally, people with bipolar disorder do not swing evenly back and forth from manic to depressive states. More often than not, the cycles of mania and depression are unpredictable and can last for very different lengths of time. You can even experience both at the same time. Many people with bipolar disorder have extreme cycles only once every few years. Yet rapid cyclers go through four or more episodes of mania and depression each year. Ultrarapid cyclers have episodes within a week, and ultradian cyclers have distinct mood swings within just twenty-four hours.

At the same time, some manic-depressives may go for weeks, months, or even years without experiencing any extreme ups and downs. Instead, they have normal moods as does everyone around them. Psychiatrists call this euthymia. A milder form of bipolar disorder is called hypomania. A hypomanic episode will leave you feeling suddenly energized, outgoing, extremely happy, and enthusiastic. Hypomanic phases are never so severe that they will seriously disrupt your life. However, even though they feel good, they are eventually followed by depression.

Who Gets Bipolar Disorder?

Bipolar disorder is often a hereditary disease, meaning that it runs in the family. However, just because one of your relatives has it does not necessarily mean that you will get it, too. Although young children can be diagnosed with manic depression, the illness more frequently appears in young adults and continues throughout life. Teenage boys and girls are equally likely to experience bipolar disorder, but it is often more apparent in girls. This is because girls tend to find it easier to talk about their feelings than do boys.

Sometimes, boys feel that admitting to being depressed means that they are weak and have no control. They tend to suppress or hold back their feelings. In the long run, this only makes life more painful and difficult.

Chapter 2

Symptoms of Bipolar Disorder

Bipolar disorder is often difficult to diagnose. Frequently, when the illness first appears, both manic and depressive phases might be somewhat mild. Teens might feel irritated, anxious, or aggressive without knowing why. A real clue is if you start behaving hyperactively or as if you have too much energy.

Because these symptoms change and are not very obvious early on, both you and those around you—even your doctor—might blame something else for your moods and difficult behavior. According to statistics, two out of three times doctors initially fail to recognize the symptoms of bipolar disorder. Also, when manic-depressives are in a milder manic phase—full of happiness, energy, and confidence—they and the people around them never stop to think that anything is wrong.

Manic depression is hard to recognize. It should be diagnosed by a psychiatrist, a doctor who specializes in the diagnosis, treatment, and prevention of mental and emotional disorders.

Depression vs. Being a "Typical" Teenager

Many of the symptoms of depression resemble the normal moods and feelings that adolescents experience. This is another reason why depression is hard to diagnose. As you grow and your body changes, the levels of hormones (chemicals in your brain and bloodstream) increase and sometimes set your body chemistry out of whack. These chemical imbalances can leave you feeling stressed out, sad, or extremely emotional. This is natural. For the most part, it is also usually temporary. However, if such feelings are very intense and keep lasting day after day, you might be depressed.

Roberto had always had times when, for no apparent reason, he felt sad. As a small child, his parents' friends made remarks such as, "Roberto's such a serious boy!"

When Roberto became an adolescent, his dad was always telling him to "lighten up," and his mother used to muss his hair in an irritating way and call him "Grumpy Face." Roberto did not know what was wrong. Then, in his second year of high school, he started having days when he didn't feel like getting out of bed.

Roberto went to school and came home as usual, but he felt as if he were living under a dark cloud. Nothing meant anything. After weeks of feeling this way, he started wondering if this was more than just a phase. Maybe he was really depressed.

Teens often realize that they are depressed before their parents or teachers suspect any problems. If you pay attention to your feelings, you can play a big role in taking care of yourself. Ask yourself the following questions: How extreme are the bad moods I have been experiencing? How long have I been having them, and how are they interfering with my day-to-day life? If they have been going on for more than a couple of weeks and are making it hard for you to function, you should definitely speak to an adult whom you trust and who can help you.

Are You Depressed?

If you are concerned that you are depressed or that someone close to you is experiencing a form of depression, you may want to take a close look at the following questions. Do you or does someone you know seem to:

◎ **Feel sad and anxious?**

◎ **Feel like a loser or feel responsible for things that go wrong?**

◎ **Get irritated by the slightest thing?**

◎ Tend to overeat or perhaps feel unable to eat at all?

◎ Have no hope for the future?

◎ Have trouble enjoying things that used to be pleasurable?

◎ Feel weak or tired?

◎ Sleep too much or not enough?

◎ Have little self-control?

◎ Cut classes, skip meetings and activities, and avoid social events?

◎ Drink or take drugs, hoping to feel better?

◎ Find it difficult to concentrate or make decisions?

◎ Feel a lack of control?

◎ Have frequent headaches or stomachaches?

◎ Frequently think about or talk about death, suicide, or self-injury?

If the answer was yes to four or more of these questions and you have had these symptoms for more than two weeks, you might be seriously depressed. If you suspect that a friend or sibling is depressed, speak to a school counselor or an adult whom you can trust and let him or her know about your concerns.

You needn't be embarrassed about seeing a counselor or therapist. These professionals can help people handle life's problems. Many people are in therapy these days.

Mania

Mania is a state of high, unnatural excitement. If you are in a manic phase, you tend to become hyperactive, overflowing with nonstop energy. Often, having so much energy can leave you feeling worried or anxious. Mania can also lead to panic attacks, during which you become immobilized (unable to take action) because you fear anything and everything. During a panic attack, even a simple choice, such as deciding to turn on the television, can cause you anxiety. In extreme cases, you might experience hallucinations or hear voices.

One day, Janice was going home on the bus. There was a lot of traffic, and the bus seemed to be taking forever. Janice started getting nervous as more and more people got on. Then everything around her went foggy. She suddenly felt over-come by anxiety. Her heart was pounding, and she started sweating. The other passengers seemed to be closing in around her. The panic inside her was so great that she started to cry.

Sometimes a manic episode can make you obsessive. You may become overwhelmed with awful thoughts or desires. Other times, you might become compulsive and feel driven to do something—such as drink, smoke, or eat—by an inner force that seems stronger than your own will. This behavior can be dangerous, causing you to feel as if you have no control over yourself.

Are You Manic?

Take a look at the list below and ask yourself these questions. Do you or does someone you know:

- Seem to need almost no sleep at all?
- Become easily distracted?
- Feel hyperalert and supersensitive?
- Fidget and move around constantly?
- Act obnoxiously?
- Talk a lot and very quickly?
- Feel on top of the world?
- Become very irritable for no reason?
- Have trouble making decisions?
- Pull dangerous stunts and act invincible?
- Feel full of creative energy?
- Come up with lots of wild and impractical ideas?
- Drink and do drugs excessively?

If the answer is yes to four or more of these questions and you have been feeling these symptoms for more than two weeks, you might be experiencing a manic episode.

Although depression might appear to be the more serious of the two phases, the manic phase is usually more dangerous. When you are manic, you might stay awake for days or even weeks at a time. Although you feel as if you are bursting with energy, your nonstop activity will eventually drain your body's energy reserves, leaving you weak, exhausted, and possibly even dehydrated. With your body's defenses down, you risk catching an infectious disease that a healthy body can normally fight off.

At the same time, when you are experiencing a manic episode, your sense of judgment and reality goes out the window. This can lead to all sorts of excessive behavior, such as gambling and spending sprees, drinking and drug taking, and promiscuous sex and physical risk taking—speeding in a car, for example. The results of such activities—unplanned pregnancies, the risk of sexually transmitted diseases, maxed-out credit cards or a loss of funds, getting kicked out of school or fired from a job, troubles with the police, alienation from friends and family—can wreck a person's life.

Chapter 3

What Causes Bipolar Disorder?

Scientists do not know exactly what causes bipolar disorder. However, most agree that the condition is due to certain chemical imbalances in the brain. This is why manic depression is considered a real physiological condition and not simply a psychological illness. Episodes of mania or depression can be brought on or aggravated by a combination of the four major factors discussed in the following sections.

Biochemical Factors

Studies show that some depressive disorders—bipolar disorder in particular—are caused by chemical imbalances in the brain. Your brain produces and uses chemicals called neurotransmitters, which send messages through your nerve cells to your entire body.

Many depressive disorders are caused by chemical imbalances in the body or brain, and can be controlled with medications that have manageable side effects.

People experiencing mania usually have too many neurotransmitters being produced, whereas people in a depressed cycle often have too few. Such excesses or deficiencies upset the communication between your brain and your body. Although much about neuro-transmitters is still being researched by scientists, once an imbalance is detected, doctors are often able to readjust levels with the use of medicine.

Genetic Factors

If there is a history of depression in your family, this can increase your chance of developing bipolar disorder. Scientists believe that there might be genes that can be inherited that make you more susceptible to manic depression. However, just because someone in your family has manic depression does not mean that you will acquire it. Also, many people with bipolar disorder come from families with no history of depression.

Environmental Factors

Your environment is made up of the things you do, the people with whom you interact, and the spaces you inhabit on a daily basis. There will always be some aspects of your environment that you will have no control over. When this happens, it is easy to feel overwhelmed and anxious. It might be a bully at school who always picks on you, your parents who fight a lot, or the death of a close friend or relative. Peer pressure,

The death of a friend or loved one can cause depression. Medication and counseling help mental illnesses caused by environmental factors as well as those that are inherited.

financial troubles at home, sickness, and divorce are other events that can leave you feeling very unhappy.

When you are under pressure, your body tries to help you by producing large amounts of certain hormones. As do neurotransmitters, hormones carry messages between your brain and your nerve cells. When you are anxious or afraid, you will often have excess amounts of a stress hormone called cortisol. Many depressed people often have higher than normal levels of cortisol. If these high levels stay in your body for a long time, they can have an effect on both your brain and your nerve cells. The changes that result can lead to serious depression.

Psychological Factors

Regardless of biochemical and genetic factors, your attitude can affect the way that a depressive illness affects you. If you tend to look at things negatively, if you lack self-confidence, and if you worry too much and find it difficult to talk about your problems, you will be less able to deal with the mood swings you are experiencing. You also have a stronger chance of becoming seriously depressed.

Teens who have had a difficult childhood might be more susceptible to depressive disorders. Tense family situations, major illnesses, troubles in school, and frequent moving from town to town can make you feel insecure and uncertain about the future. These things can make coping with manic depression very difficult.

Chapter 4

How to Detect Bipolar Disorder

It is often hard to detect bipolar disorder. What makes diagnosis particularly difficult are the manic phases associated with the disorder. When you are manic, you often feel invincible. Even if you are exhibiting classic symptoms of mania—feeling extremely uninhibited and excited—you likely won't believe anything is wrong with you.

Problems Diagnosing Teens

As we saw earlier, it is harder to detect bipolar disorder in children and teens than in adults. This is partly because adults believe it is normal for adolescents to act up, behave unpredictably, and experience mood swings. As such, symptoms of both mania and depression are often mistaken for normal teenage behavior.

Another problem is that most bipolar research is based on adult behavior, even though depressed adults often act differently than teens. While adults tend to express their depression openly, many teens hide, or repress, their depression. Often, most teens don't even know they are depressed. They just know that something is wrong. Their extreme behavior is a cry for help.

> *"I never imagined I had a real, biological problem," admits Ralph, fifteen. "All I knew was that I would get angry at people for no reason. The smallest thing could set me off. Ultimately, I think my shoplifting was just to get attention. Well, I got attention—from the cops who arrested and charged me. That's when I finally saw a psychiatrist, who discovered that I was bipolar and that I had been experiencing manic episodes. It was a relief to know that there was an explanation for my problems, and ways to treat them."*

Sadly, many parents and teachers mistakenly view teens' manic-depressive symptoms as mere bad behavior. They end up punishing teens instead of looking for the real causes of such behavior. If you aren't comfortable talking to your parents about your depression, try opening up to another adult you trust: a relative, a teacher, a coach, a close friend's parents, a clergy member, a school guidance counselor, or a social worker. If the feelings are overwhelming and don't go away, you will need to get professional help. Although bipolar disorder is a biological disease, there are no laboratory tests or other procedures, such as blood tests or brain scans, that can detect it. Instead, a doctor makes a diagnosis based on the presence of a combination of symptoms. To do this, he or she will talk to you and your parents to compile a detailed history of your symptoms, both past and present. Doctors focus on five areas when making a diagnosis:

◎ **Development: Did you have an easy birth? Were you a healthy baby who had no problems learning to walk or talk?**

◎ **Physical health: Were you a healthy child? Did you have any illnesses, accidents, surgery, or medical conditions?**

◎ **Psychological health: As a child, were you relaxed or anxious, shy or aggressive? Did you act up?**

◎ **Education: Have you always done well in school or have you had difficulty? Do you have trouble paying attention in class?**

◎ **Family: How do you get along with your parents and siblings? Are there any cases**

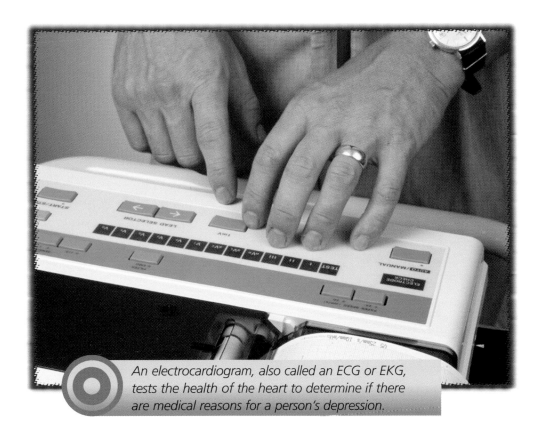

An electrocardiogram, also called an ECG or EKG, tests the health of the heart to determine if there are medical reasons for a person's depression.

of mood disorders, learning disabilities, or alcoholism in your family?

You should have a normal physical examination as well as blood and urine tests and an electrocardiogram so that a doctor can rule out any kind of medical reason for your symptoms of depression. Often, psychological tests can help give doctors additional information about your state of mind. You might be shown pictures or images, such as Rorschach inkblots, and be asked to give your interpretation of them. Your impressions may give doctors insights into your fears and concerns.

Chapter 5

The Impact of Bipolar Disorder

Bipolar disorder can affect you in many different ways. It can cause you to experience certain sensations and to behave or act in various ways. Some of these sensations and reactions are common to all kinds of depressive disorders, but others are specific to manic depression. In particular, they are the result of the manic aspects of the disease.

Creativity

Vincent Van Gogh, the Dutch painter, had five siblings; three had severe emotional problems, and one of them committed suicide. Van Gogh himself was a manic-depressive who experienced severe mood swings. It is documented that he sliced off his ear during a fit of despair. This extreme act was probably a result of his condition. When Van Gogh was depressed, he felt like an outcast and a failure. He began painting after he was unable to succeed at any other career. He created some of

Scholars think that brilliant artist Vincent Van Gogh (1853–1890) suffered from manic depression. He painted some 2,200 works, including this self-portrait.

his finest work when he was in the midst of a manic episode. During one seventy-day period in France, he completed seventy paintings—one a day!

Like Van Gogh, many great artists found outlets for their extreme feelings and heightened perceptions through art. The novelists Mark Twain and Virginia Woolf, the poets Lord Byron and Edgar Allan Poe, the artist Michelangelo, the playwright Tennessee Williams, and the composer Robert Schumann all suffered from bipolar disorder. This is not just a coincidence. Scientists believe that there is a link between creativity and manic depression. Recent studies indicate that during manic episodes, people tend to have a high creative output.

Drug and Alcohol Abuse

Another common effect of bipolar disorder is drug and alcohol use. Most often this is to dull the extreme moods experienced during both manic and depressive phases. Teenagers are particularly likely to turn to either or both substances for comfort. They are juggling the confusing symptoms of bipolar disorder as well as peer pressure to drink and do drugs. However, these substances do not make you better; all they do is temporarily mask your symptoms. Over time, they make your symptoms worse. Drugs and alcohol can act on your brain's neurotransmitters in a way that overstimulates the nerve cell pathways that govern your emotions. This can upset your natural mood-balancing systems, causing you to experience even more severe mood swings.

Many sufferers of depression turn to drugs and alcohol to cope with their feelings of inadequacy and despair.

"I started drinking and doing drugs because I did not know who I was anymore," confesses Moss, seventeen. "My mood swings left me feeling as if I couldn't relate to anybody. I felt isolated. When I got high or drunk, it seemed like I could get along better with people. My friends thought I was out of control. So I drank more. It was a vicious cycle. Then one time, I OD'd and ended up being hospitalized. Afterward, I went into a detoxification program, which has helped me stay away from drugs and alcohol. Now I'm on medication for manic depression, but I also go to Alcoholics Anonymous to help me stay clean."

The National Institute of Mental Health (NIMH) has found that abuse of alcohol and cocaine is high among manic-depressives. This is not surprising if you consider that manic-depressives not only often have a family history of mood disorders, but are also likely to have a family history of alcoholism. In fact, according to the NIMH, 60 percent of people who are found to have bipolar disorder are also diagnosed with drug or alcohol abuse.

What complicates matters is that the symptoms of bipolar disorder and substance abuse are similar, particularly manic symptoms such as feelings of invincibility and irritability, the inability to make rational judgments, and extreme highs. Doctors often have a tough time diagnosing what the primary problem is: manic depression, alcoholism, or drug addiction. This can affect how doctors treat patients. They might work on curing the addiction before dealing with the mood swings, they might stabilize the mood swings before attacking the substance abuse, or they might treat both at the same time.

Suicide

Teens who suffer from bipolar disorder are often at risk for suicidal behavior. A combination of many factors—depression, substance addiction, stress, an unhappy family situation, and difficulties with peers—can increase the risks of you thinking about, attempting, and committing suicide. Suicide is the third leading cause of death among young people between fifteen and twenty-four. Some studies show that close to 11 percent of high school students admit to having tried at least once to kill themselves. Statistically speaking, every day an average of eighteen teens commit suicide in the United States.

Severe depression, with its feelings of overwhelming hopelessness and loneliness, can make teens vulnerable to suicide. In fact, people who suffer from bipolar disorder are thirty times more likely to commit suicide than those without a mood disorder. When coupled with substance abuse and aggressive behavior, the risks for suicide grow even higher. Sadly, between 20 to 50 percent of manic-depressives attempt suicide at least once.

It is tragic when depressed teens choose this permanent solution to solve a temporary problem. Killing yourself is a mistake you can't learn from, and the one sure thing about life is that things are always bound to change. Bipolar disorder can be treated, and most of those diagnosed with the illness find a suitable treatment and go on to live healthy, stable lives.

When you're alone with your problems, they often seem a lot worse. That is why it is very important to make an effort to talk about your problems. Don't be afraid that people will think you are weak because you are depressed and need help. Talking about your problems and seeking help means taking responsibility for yourself. This shows a lot of strength. Knowing that you are not alone and that people can and want to help you is one of the best protections against suicidal thoughts.

Chapter 6

Treatments for Bipolar Disorder

According to the National Institute of Mental Health, 8.3 percent of American adolescents suffer from some form of depression. Unfortunately, statistics also show that two-thirds of depressed people never seek treatment for their disorders. This is particularly true in the case of teens with manic depression.

Depression can leave you feeling so down and hopeless that getting help seems impossible. Meanwhile, common manic sensations of euphoria and extreme self-confidence leave you feeling on top of the world. In between both mood extremes, days, months, and even years can go by during which you feel normal.

John, nineteen, remembers the first signs of bipolar disorder. "I must have been thirteen and I went around for a couple of weeks feeling really depressed. I could barely get out of bed in the morning. My mom worried, but my dad said it was just my hormones acting up. He said he had been a moody adolescent, too.

"Well, sure enough the depression passed. It wasn't until six months later that I spent a week feeling so hyper that I couldn't sleep or even sit still. However, that manic week passed, too. It took four more years and lots of ups and downs before I finally saw a psychiatrist and discovered that my moods were more than just a few hormones acting up."

Often, the person best equipped to discover that something is wrong is you. If your extreme moods are beginning to interfere with your life, start keeping a daily journal in which you record your feelings. Rereading the journal over time can help you put your behavior into perspective. If your reactions worry you, try to get some help. Like cancer, manic depression is a serious illness. If you discovered that you had cancer, you wouldn't wait for it to go away or try to cure it yourself—you would see a doctor. The same goes for bipolar disorder.

While bipolar disorder is a chronic disease with no cure, ongoing, carefully monitored treatment can control almost all symptoms and allow you to lead a full life. It is essential, however, that you get a proper diagnosis as soon as you recognize your symptoms.

According to the NIMH, an estimated 20 to 40 percent of adolescents who fail to treat major depression develop bipolar disorder within five years. So early detection is important. As with cancer, the earlier you begin treatment, the better.

As we saw in chapter 4, adolescents often experience both depression and manic depression in ways that are quite different from adults. Diagnosing, treating, and monitoring teens with manic depression therefore requires specific expertise. When getting professional help, make sure the psychiatrist and other doctors you consult have experience working with depressed adolescents.

Professional Help

You can turn to several different professionals for advice and treatment. The following list describes physicians' areas of expertise and ways in which they can help:

◎ **General physicians (such as your family doctor) can diagnose your condition and then refer you to a specialist.**

◎ **Clinical social workers are specially trained to deal with emotional disorders. They can counsel and educate you and your family.**

◎ Psychiatric nurse practitioners specialize in dealing with people with emotional
   disorders. They can give you tests, diagnose your depression, and provide medication and therapy.

◎ Psychotherapists can help you cope with
   your feelings and symptoms.

◎ Clinical psychologists can test you,
   diagnose your depression, and also
   provide therapy.

◎ Psychiatrists are medical doctors who
   specialize in mental health. They can
   test you, diagnose your depression, and
   provide medication and therapy.

There are two stages involved in treating bipolar
disorder: acute and preventive.

Acute-stage treatment aims at controlling and ending temporary manic, hypomanic, depressive, or
mixed episodes. Once the episodes are under control,
preventive-stage treatment aims to keep them from
happening again. Preventive-stage treatment is long-
term and ongoing.

During both of these stages, treatment consists of
three parts:

◉ Medication: Prescribed drugs that can control both manic and depressive symptoms.

◉ Psychotherapy: Counseling that helps you and your family to deal with the problematic feelings and behavior caused by manic depression.

◉ Education: Opportunites for you and your family to learn all about bipolar disorder and the ways to cope with it.

Types of Medication

There are three important types of medication used to treat bipolar disorder: mood stabilizers, antidepressants, and antipsychotic drugs.

Mood Stabilizers

Mood stabilizers provide relief from extreme manic or depressive episodes. One of the oldest and most commonly used mood stabilizers is a naturally occuring element called lithium. Lithium works especially well for people who experience pure manic episodes. When it is taken with other medication, it is also effective against depression. However, the trouble with lithium is that too much can be toxic and too little can prove ineffective.

To make sure your dosage is not harmful you will need to have regular blood tests. The quantity of lithium you can take also depends on the side effects it produces. These may include gastrointestinal problems, weight gain, tremors, and fatigue. Luckily, there are other medications that you can take to diminish these and other side effects.

Another mood stabilizer that works well for many different kinds of manic episodes is Depakote, which is made from a substance called valproic acid.

Other medications that have not yet been approved by the Federal Drug Administration (FDA) are also being used to treat manic depression. One of the most successful of these is Tegretol. Others include Lamictal, which has been especially useful against depression; Neurontin, which reduces anxiety; and Topomax, which works well against mania. Studies have shown that one out of three people with bipolar disorder will experience no symptoms at all if they take mood stabilizers on a regular basis.

Though these medications may be taken on their own, they are most often combined with each other or with other medications. But since all these medications have side effects, they need to be carefully monitored. For example, recent studies have indicated that mood stabilizers containing valproic acid may cause hormonal problems in girls if dosages are not carefully controlled.

Antidepressants

Antidepressants are used to treat the depressive phases of bipolar disorder. They are almost always prescribed with mood stabilizers because on their own they can push you into a manic state. The most commonly prescribed antidepressants include Prozac, Zoloft, Wellbutrin, Effexor, and Paxil. If one drug produces uncomfortable side effects, ask your doctor to prescribe another.

Antipsychotic Drugs

If you experience very extreme mania or depression, with symptoms such as hallucinations and delusions, your doctor will probably prescribe an antipsychotic drug. Aside from calming your anxieties, antipsychotic drugs can also function as mood stabilizers.

Medication Cocktails

Treating manic depression is very complicated because what works for one person might not work for another. Also, some drugs might become less effective over time or produce side effects that are difficult to live with. The best results often come from combinations of medications. These combinations are known as med (for medication) cocktails, or simply meds. Though med cocktails can be successful, you might still experience occasional episodes of mania or depression. Furthermore, it can take weeks or even months before some drugs take full effect.

Medication is usually taken daily at specific times and in specific doses. It is extremely important to always take your medication as prescribed. Some people become lazy and begin skipping doses. Others stop taking meds because they go for a long time without experiencing their symptoms or because, in the midst of a manic episode, they feel invincible or distracted.

For whatever reason, if you suddenly stop taking strong medications—or take them at the wrong time or in the wrong quantities—you can hurt yourself. Not taking meds as directed can be dangerous or even life threatening. Not only can it trigger worse episodes of mania or depression, it can also have a serious negative impact on your delicately balanced nervous system.

For the same reasons, you should never mix your medication with any other drugs or with alcohol. Even before taking pills for a headache, vitamins, or a natural remedy, you should always check with your doctor first.

Being responsible with your medication will not only help your treatment, it will boost your self-confidence, too. You will be controlling your disease instead of letting it control you.

Start by making a schedule of when to take your medication. It is also helpful if you keep a journal or mood chart to track how you are feeling from day to day. If you notice any change at all, you should contact your doctor immediately. Remember that only you know how your drugs are making you feel and what side effects they are producing.

Psychotherapy

Seeing a psychiatrist, a psychotherapist, or another mental health specialist is another essential part of treating bipolar disorder. Psychotherapy helps you to understand the disease and learn how to cope with the feelings and behavior it can produce.

There are four main types of therapy that can help treat manic depression:

◉ **Behavioral therapy focuses on behavior that can increase or decrease stress and depression.**

◉ **Cognitive therapy focuses on identifying and changing negative ways of thinking.**

◉ **Interpersonal therapy focuses on how to improve your relationships with those around you.**

◉ **Social rhythms therapy focuses on how to organize and stick to a daily routine that stabilizes your body's rhythms.**

All of these therapies can be done individually, in a group, or with your family. Sometimes it is useful to do all three. The most important thing about therapy is that you trust and feel comfortable with your therapist. If after three sessions you feel it's not working, look for someone else. Don't give up on therapy altogether.

Sixteen-year-old Tony didn't want to see a therapist. And the first time he saw Dr. Monroe was a disaster. "I'm not going back," he swore to his parents. "The guy just sat there and eyeballed me. He never talked. Just spent all his time doodling on a pad of paper."

Tony complained to his friend Alexey about Dr. Monroe. "You shouldn't give up, Tony," said Alexey. "When my dad died, I was very depressed. I went to see this psychiatrist, Dr. Zucherman, who really helped me. He's a very caring guy and really bright. You should give him a call."

Tony figured he had nothing to lose. He called Dr. Zucherman's office and made an appointment. "Right from the first session," Tony recalled, "we got along well. I immediately trusted him and I could tell he cared about what I had to say. I've been seeing him for a year now and have made a lot of progress. I never thought I'd say this, but I actually like going to therapy."

Keep in mind that psychotherapy is not like medication. There are no overnight cures. But over time, it can really make a permanent difference in helping you to cope with your bipolar symptoms.

Education

The more you and your family know about bipolar disorder, the easier it is to deal with. Learn everything you can about the disease and ways of treating it. Read books and Web sites, ask your doctors questions, and join your local chapter of the National Depressive and Manic-Depressive Association (NDMDA) to find out how others deal with manic depression.

Remember that scientific studies are constantly discovering new things about bipolar disorder and new medications are being developed and tested all the time. Being aware of what's going on is important.

Taking Care of Yourself

An important part of living with bipolar disorder is taking care of yourself. Although professionals, friends, and family can help, you are the one who knows best what you are going through. You are the one who can best take steps to make things easiest on yourself.

A healthy body can have a really big impact on a healthy mind. Eat balanced, nutritious meals at least three times a day. Avoid alcohol, caffeine, and junk

Practicing yoga, as seen here, or getting any form of exercise can help those with mental illness maintain control over their symptoms and their health.

food because they have a lot of sugar, salt, and artificial ingredients. All of these ingredients contain chemicals that can throw your body out of whack. It is also a good idea to drink a lot of water, which has many health benefits and helps to prevent dehydration (sometimes a side effect of bipolar medications).

Exercise is also key. Among other benefits, it helps to release stress and tension. Exercise gives you a jump-start when you are feeling unmotivated, and provides you with a healthy outlet if you are suddenly flooded with manic energy. Choose a sport or an activity that you enjoy and that is not too complicated to do. This way you can stick with it and make it a scheduled part of your life.

Stress can be part of anybody's life, but too much neglected tension can aggravate or set off episodes of mania or depression. Aside from medication and therapy, it is very important to learn to deal with stress.

Part of dealing with stress is learning how to relax. Relaxing is often more difficult than it seems. It takes some practice and concentration. Allow yourself plenty of downtime to kick back and watch a movie, ride a bike, or hang out with a good pal.

Most important, be good to yourself. Even if you sometimes feel weak and rotten, you are going through a lot and deserve relaxation. Make sure you sleep well. When you are weak and exhausted, your physical and emotional defenses also weaken. If you are having problems sleeping, talk to your doctor, who can prescribe sleep medication.

Finally, do not be afraid to share details of your condition with family and friends. Many people do not understand manic depression. They might say things such as "It's all in your head," or "You're exaggerating." Explain it to them, and don't be afraid to talk when you are feeling alone, desperate, or suicidal. Surround yourself with good people on whom you can count. Aside from friends and family, know that there are youth groups, specialized hotlines, and associations for people who suffer from depressive disorders, including bipolar disorder.

Fourteen-year-old Sam felt as if he was sinking into a deep hole. He had never felt so hopeless. He stopped doing his homework and ignored his friends and family. Just getting out of bed took enormous effort. Life was becoming increasingly unbearable, and neither drinking nor drugs helped make him feel better. So one day, when he really couldn't stand things anymore, he swallowed a handful of his mother's prescription sleeping pills.

When Sam woke up, he was in the intensive care unit of a hospital. He had just had his stomach pumped. He remained in the hospital for two weeks, undergoing numerous physical and psychological tests. Diagnosed with major depression, he was prescribed antidepressants by a psychiatrist. The medication seemed to make a difference. Sam felt a cloud lifting in his head. He was released from the hospital soon after.

At home and at school, everyone was nice to Sam. But he felt that they were all afraid of him, too. While he no longer felt depressed, he began to feel that his parents, his teachers, and his friends were whispering about him behind his back. He found himself lashing out at them for no reason. Sometimes he felt very anxious or panicked. He couldn't sleep and worried that the drugs weren't working. In fact, they seemed to be making him worse.

Sam's parents became alarmed at his aggressive behavior. When he was suspended from school for threatening to punch his math teacher, they took Sam to see Dr. Mader, another psychiatrist. After questioning him closely about his symptoms, Dr. Mader said that he believed Sam was manic-depressive. He said that the doctors at the hospital had only detected the depressive phase of the disease and that the antidepressants had triggered a manic episode. To stabilize Sam's moods, Dr. Mader prescribed lithium.

At first the lithium didn't seem to have any effect. But when Dr. Mader increased the dosage, Sam became so nauseous that he could not keep any food down. After experimenting with various drug combinations, Sam discovered that he reacted well to a mixture of Tegretol, antidepressants, and antipsychotics.

At the same time, he saw Dr. Mader twice a week for therapy, at first with his family, and later by himself.

Today, Sam is eighteen and he has just begun attending a university. He has a girlfriend and plans to move out and get his own apartment next year. He accepts that he is manic-depressive and will be for the rest of his life. Taking his meds is as normal to him as eating breakfast. So is seeing his therapist once a week.

Sam still has days when he feels down and others when he feels anxious and irritable. These moods sometimes overwhelm him, but at least he knows where they come from and how to cope with them. So do his family, his girl-friend, and his friends. Instead of trying to hide that he is manic-depressive, Sam has found that being open about his illness has strengthened many of his closest relationships. A few friends initially distanced themselves from him, but most have been supportive.

Although he knows his friends and family care, Sam really looks forward to his weekly sup-port group for young people with bipolar disor-der. It is a great comfort to share experiences with people his own age who have similar feel-ings and problems. It helps to know that he is not alone.

Glossary

antidepressants Medication prescribed to relieve depression. Three of the most common are Zoloft, Paxil, and Prozac.

bipolar disorder Illness in which emotions swing between two (bi) opposite (polar) emotional states. The clinical term for manic depression.

compulsiveness A psychological state of being strongly driven to do something.

Depakote A mood stabilizer used to treat manic depression.

electrocardiogram A medical procedure that shows the changes of electric potential that occur during a heartbeat.

genetic Relating to genes; something that is hereditary.

hormones Chemicals that carry messages between your brain and your nerve cells.

hyperactivity A state of being excessively active, energetic, and unable to concentrate.

hypomania A mild form of manic depression in which manic phases are less extreme.

lithium A natural substance commonly prescribed as a mood stabilizer for manic depression.

mania A psychological state in which you feel excessive energy, happiness, and enthusiasm.

neurotransmitters Chemicals that your brain uses to send messages to the rest of your body.

obsessiveness Psychological state in which you focus excessively on a single feeling or idea.

physiological Relating to the workings of the physical body.

psychological Relating to the workings of the mind.

psychotherapy Treatment of mental or emotional disorders through psychological analysis.

Rorschach inkblot test A psychological test in which you interpret abstract ink patterns.

Tegretol A mood stabilizer used to treat manic depression.

Where to Go for Help

In the United States

American Psychiatric Association
1400 K Street NW, Suite 1101
Washington, DC 20005
(888) 357-7924
Web site: http://www.psych.org

Lithium Information Center
Madison Institute of Medicine
7617 Mineral Point Road, Suite 300
Madison, WI 53717
(608) 827-2470
Web site: http://www.miminc.org/aboutlithinfoctr.html

National Alliance for the Mentally Ill (NAMI)
Colonial Place Three, 2107 Wilson Boulevard, Suite 300
Arlington, VA 22201
(800) 950-6264
Web site: http://www.nami.org

National Depressive and Manic-Depressive
   Association (NDMDA)
730 North Franklin Street, Suite 501
Chicago, IL 60610-7204
(800) 826-3632
Web site: http://www.ndmda.org

National Foundation for Depressive Illness
P.O. Box 2257
New York, NY 10116
(800) 239-1265
Web site: http://www.depression.org

National Institute of Mental Health (NIMH)
6001 Executive Boulevard, R. 8184, MSC 9663
Bethseda, MD 20892-9663
(301) 4443-4513
Web site: http://www.nimh.nih.gov

National Mental Health Association
1021 Prince Street
Alexandria, VA 22314
(800) 969-NMHA
Web site: http://www.nmha.org

In Canada

Canadian Mental Health Association
CMHA Ontario Division
180 Dundas Street West, Suite 2301

59

Toronto, ON M5G 1Z8
(416) 977-5580
(800) 875-6213
Web site: http://www.ontario.cmha.ca

Centre for Addiction and Mental Health (CAMH)
33 Russell Street
Toronto, ON M5S 2S1
(416) 535-8501 ext. 6048
e-mail: foundation@camh.net
Web site: http://www.camh.net/

The Mood Disorders Association of Ontario
40 Orchard View Boulevard, Suite 222
Toronto, ON M4R 1B9
(416) 486-8046
(888) 486-8236
Web site: http://www.mooddisorders.on.ca

Web Sites

Due to the changing nature of Internet links, the Rosen Publishing Group, Inc., has developed an online list of Web sites related to the subject of this book. This site is updated regularly. Please use this link to access the list:

http://www.rosenlinks/ntk/bidi/

For Further Reading

Cobain, Bev. *When Nothing Matters Anymore: A Survival Guide for Depressed Teens.* Minneapolis, MN: Free Spirit, 1998.

Duke, Patty, and Gloria Hockman. *A Brilliant Madness: Living with Manic Depressive Illness.* New York: Bantam Books, 1993.

Eshom, Daniel B. *Lithium: What You Should Know.* New York: The Rosen Publishing Group, Inc., 1998.

Gelman, Amy. *Coping with Depression.* New York: The Rosen Publishing Group, Inc., 1998.

Jamison, Kay Redfield. *An Unquiet Mind: A Memoir of Moods and Madness.* New York: Alfred A. Knopf, 1995.

Nelson, Richard E., and Judith C. Galas. *The Power to Prevent Suicide: A Guide for Teens Helping Teens.* Minneapolis, MN: Free Spirit, 1994.

Silverstein, Alvin, Virginia Silverstein, and Laura Silverstein Nunn. *Depression.* Springfield, NJ: Enslow Publishing, 1997.

Index

Credits

About the Author

Michael Sommers is a freelance author who has a master's degree in history and civilization.

Photo Credits

Cover photo by Les Mills; pp. 2, 35 © Corbis; p. 13 by Maura Boruchow; p. 17 by Ethan Zindler; pp. 21, 28 by Thaddeus Harden; pp. 26, 33 © Custom Medical; p. 37 by Antonio Mari; p. 51 by Brian Silak.

Design and Layout

Thomas Forget